How to Grow Microgreens

For Fun or Profit

By Practicalgrowing.com

Table of Contents

Introduction

Do you enjoy seeing plants grow? Do you often find yourself looking for new ways to make your diet healthier? If you find yourself answering yes to both questions, then you have chosen the right book!

In this book, you are going to learn how to grow microgreens. I will talk about how to grow this superfood for fun and to add their great nutritional benefits to your diet. I will also explain how to grow these plants to make a profit as a side hustle or full-time business.

We will start by looking into what microgreens are and why you should consider growing them. Then, we will talk about the different ways in which microgreens can be enjoyed. You will learn all the technical terms that you need to know and understand in order to get started on your journey.

We will then explore the different types of microgreens. We will learn about which types are easy to grow and which are more difficult to grow. This information will help you to choose which type of microgreen to start with based on your skill level.

Once we learn all about what microgreens are and the other background information we need, we will start to dive into the actual process of growing microgreens.

I will tell you what you need to know to start growing them, from the supplies to the different growing techniques, and what kind of space you need in your home to grow microgreens.

We will discuss temperature, watering, humidity, airflow and more to make sure that you can have the greatest level of success in your growing journey.

We will then talk about when and how to harvest your microgreens.

If you are looking to make a profit from microgreens, we will move into talking about the business side of things.

We will go into detail on the most important things to know before you start to sell your microgreens like:

- Food safety
- Government rules
- How to certify yourself as an organic grower
- Testing seeds
- Packaging your microgreens
- Deciding the price
- Calculating costs
- Marketing and sales

We will finish up by covering a few FAQ's that may be beneficial for you if you run into trouble while growing your microgreens.

Growing Microgreens for Fun

What are Microgreens?

Microgreens are a new nutritional trend that is commonly being grown and eaten today. They are pretty simple when you actually look into what they are.

They are simply seedlings of plants. Microgreens are harvested before they have the chance to grow into a mature plant. They are typically harvested between one and three weeks after they emerge from their seed.

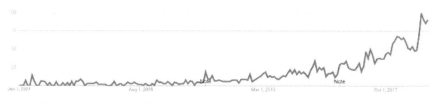

Popularity according to Google for the term 'microgreens'

To give you a better example of what microgreens are like, let's compare microgreens and sprouts. Sprouts are a nutritionally dense food that has been commonly eaten for many years.

Sprouts are grown in a humid environment, for example in a sprouting jar. They are consumed before they reach the microgreen stage. No soil or growing media is used.

Sprouts

Microgreens are grown in soil or another growing media. Microgreens are also harvested from a much wider variety of plants than sprouts are.

Microgreens

Microgreens can be eaten on their own but typically people add them into their food as decoration. This is because the taste can be quite strong.

Some common ways that microgreens are consumed is in soups, salads, smoothies, and juices.

They can be added to salads, you can blend them to make a smoothie or turn them into a juice. There are many ways to use microgreens, so just about anyone can benefit from them.

Salad dressed with microgreens

Now that we know what microgreens are, let's investigate why you should consider growing them.

First, they are simply fun to grow. They can be grown indoors, where you can watch your seeds turn into healthy microgreens rather quickly.

They are small so they do not take up much space in your home. They are also very easy to grow. This is because you harvest microgreens so early that you do not need to worry about being able to keep the plant alive for long.

Microgreens are also great to grow because they are healthy superfoods. If you grow them in your home, you will always have them to throw on top of a salad or blend into a smoothie. It adds a convenient way to get extra vitamins, antioxidants, and nutrients into your daily diet.

Another reason to grow microgreens is for the profit that they can make you. They have a fast turnaround because they grow so quickly and they have a good return on investment or ROI. Health-conscious people are willing to pay a premium for the already grown microgreens. We will investigate this information in greater detail in the second section of this book, though. For this section, we are going to focus on growing microgreens for fun.

Stall selling microgreens

Next, let's look deeper into some different terms and definitions that you will need to know before you start your journey with microgreens.

Sprouts

The first term that you will need to know about is sprouts. As we mentioned earlier, sprouts are like microgreens, but they are not the same thing. The first difference between these two superfoods is how each of them is grown. Sprouts are grown in humid conditions while microgreens are grown in soil or substrate.

The second difference is that sprouts and microgreens are harvested at different times in the growing cycle. Sprouts are harvested immediately after the seed sprouts out of its hull. This usually happens around four to seven days after the seed is soaked in water.

Typical sprouting jar

Microgreens

Microgreens, on the other hand, are harvested a bit later. They are harvested after the little plant gets its first set of leaves (cotyledon) or true leaves (depending on the desired taste). This usually takes one to three weeks from when the seed was sown.

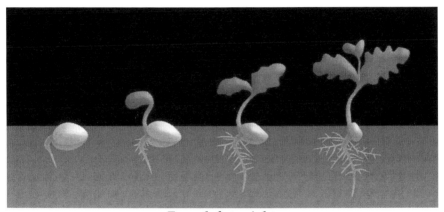

From left to right:
seed, sprout, cotyledon stage, true leaf stage

Shoots

Shoots get confused with microgreens all the time. Shoots are just bigger microgreens. For example, sunflower microgreens are one of the largest microgreens. That's why people sometimes refer to them as sunflower shoots.

Baby Greens

Baby greens are yet another type of young plant that is harvested early for their nutritional benefits. Baby greens are different from sprouts and microgreens. They are typically harvested at the latest stage of all the superfoods that come from immature plants. They are harvested when they have a few sets of leaves which normally occur around 20 to 40 days after the seed was planted.

Mature Greens

Mature greens are the leafy green vegetables that you are used to seeing. They include plants like spinach, lettuce, and kale. These greens are grown to full maturity before they are harvested. They still contain great nutritional value and they are what you would typically see people using to make salads.

Now that we have covered the growing stages of a plant, let's look back to why you got this book; microgreens.

Microgreens can be grown from a wide variety of plants. Some microgreens that are easy to grow and that can be harvested quickly are:

- Arugula
- Sunflower
- Kale
- Radish
- Broccoli
- Mustard
- Pak Choy
- Komatsuna
- Cress
- Lettuce
- Red-Veined Sorrel
- Wheatgrass
- Pea

Some microgreens that are more challenging to grow are:

- Amaranth
- Beet
- Swiss Chard
- Cilantro
- Basil
- Dill
- Carrots
- Scallions
- Purslane

The most used and sold microgreens are: (not in order)

- Sunflower
- Pea
- Radish
- Broccoli
- Wheatgrass
- Arugula
- Alfalfa
- Beet

Once you start looking into the details of microgreens, they are easy to understand. They are just plants harvested when they are very young. They are in-between sprouts and baby greens. They can be grown from many different types of seeds and plants. They take up little space in your home and provide great nutrition to your daily diet.

Now that we know all about what microgreens are, let's learn what equipment you will need to grow them.

Equipment needed

Seeds

First, you need seeds. You obviously won't be able to grow anything without these! So, when you begin the growing process for microgreens, think of which plants you would like to grow. Look back to the list of plants that we provided in the previous chapter and choose a few that look interesting to you. I recommend trying an easy one first. For example broccoli, cauliflower, cabbage, mustard, chia, sunflower or buckwheat.

Once you choose the seeds you would like, you can order them online from sites like:

- highmowingseeds.com
- trueleafmarket.com
- johnnyseeds.com
- and many others

I don't have experience ordering from a nearby gardening store. I have found it more convenient to order online. These online companies are specialized in microgreen seeds, so I just go with them. They are cheaper when you order in bulk.

Grow media

Your microgreens don't need nutrients to grow because all the required nutrients are coming from the seeds. That's why it's a waste of money to use expensive fertilizer or other mixes that use added fertilizer.

The simplest soil to use is a regular germination mix or a seed starting mix. This is a good choice for beginners because it is a product that everyone is familiar with and it is even a product that you may have laying around in your garden shed or garage. It mainly consists of a mixture of peat moss and vermiculite/perlite.

Example of a seed starting mix

Basically, you are looking at a growing media that:

- Is fluffy
- Retains water
- Doesn't have large particles in it

You could also grow your microgreens in coco coir. When you buy it, it comes in dried compressed blocks. You need to break apart the blocks into finer fluffy material in order to use it.

You can also let it soak for about an hour to break it apart more easily. This can be a time-consuming task if you are growing commercially.

Coco coir makes a great growing media because it can hold a large amount of water. The good thing about coco coir is that it's sustainable while peat moss is not. Make sure you have a proper drain tray because the water that is draining trough will be brown.

Coco Coir bricks

A DIY composting mix (soilless mix) is another option. Fellow growers have reported to me that they are using the following mix:

- 2 parts screened compost
- 2 parts coco coir or peat moss
- 1 part perlite

Here is another DIY potting mix with a little bit more perlite. If your mix gets dry quickly you can use this mixing ratio:

- 1 part screened compost
- 1 part coco coir or peat moss
- 1 part perlite

You can adjust these according to your own experiments and germination rates.

Once you have made your own mix or have bought a commercial seed germination or potting mix you can test it using the following method:

Lower than 80% germination? → add some moisture-retaining medium like peat moss, coco coir or vermiculite.

Not draining properly? → too much moisture in the soil. Decrease the amount of moisture-retaining medium.

If you choose to grow your microgreens with hydroponics, you will want to use bio felt or biostrate for your growing media. This will provide the perfect atmosphere for your microgreens to grow.

Bio felt, also known as biostrate.
Mainly used in hydroponic setups (no soil)

Another hydroponics setup with Biofelt

I will talk more about hydroponic growing later in the book.

Trays or Flats

You will need trays to put your growing media in as well. The best type of trays to buy for microgreen growing is the 10x20x1 inch trays that have holes in the bottom. These are a good size for microgreens as the roots do not have the time to grow very deep. You can put many seeds in a tray of this size. The holes in the bottom of the tray help with drainage in case you ever happen to overwater your plants.

This size is the industry standard. If you hear people talking about what their seed density is, they are referring to the density in a 10x20 flat.

A classic 10x20x1 inch growing flat

Some people prefer 10x20x2 flats which are one inch higher. These flats help to keep the dirt in and help support the microgreens that are growing on the sides. If you are growing indoors and don't want to make a mess, I would recommend using these. Harvesting the microgreens can be a bit tougher on the 2-inch-high trays because you must reach in and cut them in the tray instead of on top of the tray.

If you are growing microgreens as a hobby you can use the 10x10x1 or 10x10x2. This is half the size of the 'standard' flat but still big enough to get you enough microgreens. You just need to divide the weight of the seeds by two to get the proper seeding density (more on seeding density later).

A 10x10x2 tray

It's best to order thick trays because the thin ones can break very easily. Thin ones get flimsy when they are exposed to the sun.

If you can only find trays without holes you can simply drill holes in them yourself. Stack 5 trays on top of each other and drill a fair number (10+) of holes for the water to drain out of. Make sure you have some without holes to act as drip trays or as blackout domes.

If you are running an indoor system, you can use a tray without holes on the bottom and a growing tray with holes on the top. This is to avoid spilling any water from overwatering on the floor or on other microgreens below. This is called a 'drip tray'.

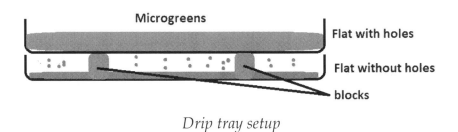

Drip tray setup

The 'blocks' in the diagram can be anything. If you are using the drip tray method, I recommend using bamboo or rocks as the 'block' material.

Growing rack

You don't necessarily need a rack if you want to grow a few trays, but if you are running a commercial operation or just want to grow more you, it's best to use a rack.

You can move them around and place them where they can get the best light. Your local hardware store will sell steel wire racks that are easy to use while growing microgreens.

Look for a rack that is a little more than one foot in height between each level.

Steel wire rack from Home Depot

You could also make a DIY rack out of wood or PVC piping.

Seeding/harvesting table

You may want to have a seeding table for seeding and harvesting your microgreens as well. This is a big process and can take up a lot of space.

A seeding table would be a great investment to help you with planting and growing your microgreens.

You can use the same seeding table as a harvesting table too. Make sure you clean the table between the seeding and harvesting stages.

You don't need a seeding and harvesting table when you are growing for your own consumption. It's just more convenient when you are handling larger quantities of microgreens.

Lights

You can use natural sunlight in order to grow microgreens, but if you decide to grow them commercially, you will want to get some artificial lights. The price for the crop will justify the extra cost that comes with artificial lights.

The most commonly used artificial lights for microgreens are TL tubes and LEDs. The reason why high-pressure sodium light (HPS) and most others are not often used is that these lamps produce a lot of heat (high lumens), which means there needs to be a bigger gap between the crop and the light.

By using TL tubes or LEDs you can place the lights closer to the microgreens which will make the trays stackable in a rack. This will increase your yield per square foot which is very useful if you plan on growing in small spaces.

If you are growing microgreens you need to use a blue spectrum light instead of red. When growing any kind of plants, blue light is used for growth while red is used for flowering. The microgreens are harvested before they can flower so using red lights will be a waste of electricity.

There is one instance where red light might be beneficial to you. The red spectrum can be used to slow down the growth of your microgreens. This is useful when your microgreens are ready to harvest but your client needs them in 3 days. The red light will keep them fresh without letting them grow past the microgreen stage.

TL Lights
TL lights are the most common source of artificial light used by microgreen growers. They are a tested and proven method of light for microgreens. If you use TL light, you need to decide if you are going to use T5, T8, or T12 tubes.

Different TL lights

T5 is the most used light with T8 coming in second. Most of the time, they are used in a dual configuration and are four feet long. These will be enough to supply light to 4 trays (10x20x1) of microgreens. You need to repeat this setup for each level on the rack. Look for 6500K lights which are labeled as white light. The distance from the light to the plant should be about one foot.

The only disadvantage of TL lights is when one gets damaged or in the unlikely event that one explodes. If this happens you will need to throw away your whole harvest because there will be glass everywhere. Covering these with a clear plastic protective cap will solve this problem.

Growing microgreens with TL lights

LED

Some people use LED lights to grow their microgreens, they can be more expensive if you are buying from a reputable brand. However, with a top of the line LED light you can adjust the color spectrum. If you want to slow down growth because there is no customer for that crop, you can change the light spectrum to red (4000k).

LED lights are very versatile. You can adjust the brightness and color spectrum. However, all this convenience comes at a price.

Some microgreens prefer less intense light such as arugula, bok choy, and amaranth. A good way to spot if your microgreen is getting too much light is if they produce brown spots on their leaves. When you see this happening it's a good idea to add a shade cloth, reduce the light exposure time, place the lights higher, or move them to a place where they will get less direct light.

Timer

You should have your lights on for about 16 hours a day to promote the maximum growth of your microgreens. It's best to connect your lights to a 24-hour timer so you don't have to worry about turning them on and off every day. There will be a maximum rating of watts on the timer. Make sure you don't go over this rating. Combine all the watts of all your lights and check if it is under the rated watts stated on the timer. The last thing you want to develop is fire.

A 24h adjustable timer

Calculating energy cost

Let's do a quick calculation of the energy costs for your grow lights.

One T8 light that is 4 feet long will consume 16 watts. If you have a dual setup, (meaning two lights in one fixture) it will consume 32 watts, which is enough light for 4 trays. Imagine having 4 levels for a total of 16 trays and a total of 128 watts.

If you would run this setup for 16 hours a day you would require a total of:

$$128\ watts\ x\ 16\ hours = 2000\ watt\ hours\ or\ 2kWh\ per\ day$$

If you want to know the cost for one day, we multiply the kilowatt-hours per day with the price for one kilowatt per hour for your location.

$$2kWh\ x\ \$0.18\ per\ kWh = \$0.36$$

You would have to pay $0.36 in electricity costs to run your lights for 16 hours a day. You need to adjust the cost per kWh to your local rate.

Fan

You will also want to have a fan blowing near your growing space. This helps the air to move around so that the plants continue to get the fresh air that they need to grow strong stems and prevent mold.

Try to have the air blown indirectly on the microgreens. Having the air blow directly at the microgreens may cause rapid drying of the growing media.

Scale

A scale is also a helpful tool since that will help you measure your seed density in an accurate way. Make sure you note down the seed density you use in order to have the optimal harvest (more on seed density later).

Temperature and humidity meter

Another must-have item is a temperature and humidity meter. You need to have the correct values in order to grow your microgreens and prevent mold. I will talk more about this in the next chapter.

Basic temperature and humidity meter

Misting bottle

You will need a misting bottle to spray water on your seedlings after you have sown them. A misting bottle is only used in the germination stage. Afterward, you will water them from the bottom or only water the soil.

When you water your seeds with a hose or cup, the seeds will start to float which will disrupt them. That's why you need to use a misting bottle.

There are two types of misting bottles, one where you press the handle every time you spray and one where you build up pressure in the can using your hand. The first one is easy to use if you are growing for fun, but I recommend the second if you are growing larger quantities.

Handheld misting bottle with hand pump

Spice shaker

Some people have magic hands and can distribute their seeds evenly using just one cup filled with their seeds. Unfortunately, I'm not that gifted so I need some sort of shaker to distribute the seeds evenly. I use an empty spice shaker because it has some holes in it. This way, I can have an even spread of seeds.

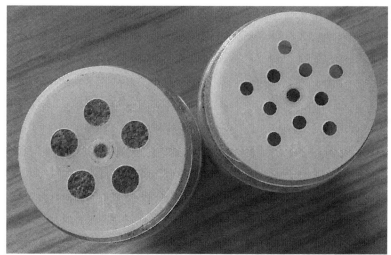

Ideal spice shaker sizes

Humidity dome

If you can't get your humidity up to 40-50% you can use a humidity dome to keep the moisture in. If you spray paint them black you can also use them as a blackout or germination dome.

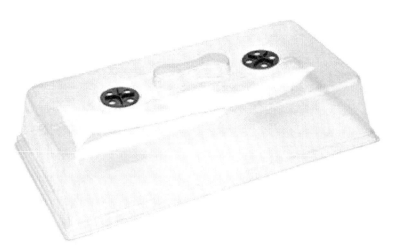

Humidity dome for 10x20 trays

Advanced Equipment

Next, let's look into some supplies that you may want to use once you become more advanced in the field of growing microgreens. You will still need the basic necessary supplies, but there are more tools available that can help you take your growing to the next level.

Heat Mats

Heat mats are a tool that can really improve growth, germination speed, and success rate of your microgreens. They help to heat your plants from the bottom of the soil to the top. This helps your plants to germinate faster and it keeps them healthier overall. Heat mats are mainly used in greenhouses where it would be costly to heat the whole greenhouse.

A standard heat mat from Amazon

Refrigeration space

You may also want a refrigeration space for your microgreens. Of course, your regular fridge can work for this, but if you grow commercially, you may need a refrigeration space dedicated to your plants. Refrigeration is used to store your microgreens once they are dried to extend their shelf life.

Harvester

If you are growing a lot of microgreens, you can even buy a machine that moves over the top of your plants and harvests the microgreens for you.

This can be a small or large harvester. The small version would be a cutting tool like a small hedge trimmer.

Small handheld hedge trimmer

If you are growing many microgreens and the labor cost of people harvesting the greens will be higher than buying an actual machine, you will need a specialized microgreen harvester like the one in the following image.

Commercial microgreens harvester

Dehumidifier

If you have a humidity level above the recommended value (40-50%) and have no option of ventilation, you should get yourself a dehumidifier. It can be turned on automatically once the air reaches a certain level and it will turn itself off once it has reached a lower level. I highly recommend it if you are growing commercially!

Make sure you get one with a hose, so you don't have to empty the water reservoir all the time (more on humidity later in the book).

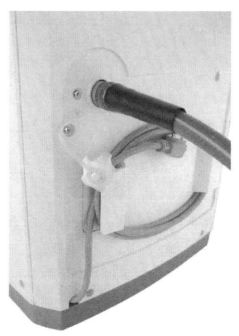

Dehumidifier with hose for worry-free drainage

Grow room

If there is no way for you to control temperature and humidity levels, the best way to grow them is by using a temperature and humidity-controlled grow room. These grow rooms are used a lot in the marijuana growing industry but can also be used for your microgreens.

A typical grow room

Make sure you get a rack that fits the grow room together with a fan to supply fresh air. If you want to go professional, you can increase the CO_2 in the air to 1000 ppm to further speed up the growing process of the microgreens. This is a technique called CO_2 enrichment which is commonly used in commercial greenhouses to speed up growth and reduce the need for moisture.

Dryer

Once you harvest your microgreens you need to wash them in cold water to rinse off the remaining seed hulls. You can dry them in a salad spinner or in a herb drying rack which are both available online.

A herb drying rack

Recap

Let's look at a quick reminder of the tools needed to grow microgreens. The basic materials needed are:

- Seeds
- Grow media
- Trays or flats
- Growing rack
- Seeding/harvesting table
- Lights
- Timer
- Fan
- Scale
- Temperature and humidity meter
- Misting bottle
- Spice shaker
- Humidity dome

Advanced equipment:

- Heat mats
- Refrigeration space
- Microgreens harvester
- Dehumidifier
- Grow room
- dryer

Growing Techniques

Soil

The technique that works best for me and most other growers is to grow them in a tray with a soil-less mix. The mix can be any kind of potting or seed starting mix we discussed earlier in this book.

This gives the plants the optimal environment that they need without the need for nutrients. It provides great results with minimal effort.

If you don't want to use a soil-less mix, the following method might be for you.

Hydroponics

Hydroponics is basically growing without soil. Since microgreens don't need nutrients to grow, you won't need to use fertilizer. You will just be borrowing the technique from hydroponics.

Advantages:
- No need to prepare the soil
- Chefs prefer bio felt instead of soil in their kitchen

Disadvantages:
- Not ideal for every type of microgreens
- Steep learning curve
- Not as much information about growing microgreens in hydroponics

I wouldn't recommend growing microgreens hydroponically. It's a steep learning curve and the disadvantages overweigh the advantages. I have tested soil vs hydroponics and from my tests, the soil was the overall winner.

Hydroponics has its place with growing fodder (wheatgrass) for animals. When you are cultivating fodder, there is no need for growing media. The roots will just grow in the trays. Which makes it fast and cheap. I tried this myself in a small setup and it's quite a fun way to grow wheatgrass.

The following picture is an example of a farm growing fodder for their animals in wintertime.

A commercial hydroponic fodder system

Additional growing information

Seeding Density

Seeding density is the weight of seeds you need to put on a certain growing area in order to have the highest yield or return on investment.

Sadly, there is no perfect seed density number that works for everybody, but there are general guidelines. You should use these guidelines to start out with and adjust your seeding density according to your own experience.

You will want to pay attention to which densities you use and the results that they yield. You should write all this information down in a notebook so that you are able to look back on it and compare results. Keep into account that different suppliers have different guidelines and seeding density rates.

The first time you plant microgreens, you will mostly be focusing on learning the steps and keeping the plants alive and healthy. Once you have done it a few times, these things will become easy and you will be able to focus more on the minor details of your growing technique.

Too dense → development of mold and diseases.
Not dense enough → no support for the microgreens and reduced yields leading to a lower return on investment.

Density by volume
You can measure by volume, which would basically just be looking at the number of seeds you use. For example, 5 tablespoons per tray. This method is not exact and not used by professional growers.

Density by weight

You can also measure by weight, which is the most accurate way to measure your seeding rates. This is the method that's most used. If you are researching seeding density you are likely to be presented with the weight per flat (10x20 inches).

This weight is the weight of the seed before being soaked.

From my own experience, people have different seeding rates for their microgreens. I have investigated many seed suppliers' lists of recommended seed density and they are all different. So, it would be impossible to give you a rule to live by. Instead, I'm going to give you a reference for small, medium and big seeds.

Small seeds: 1/8th of an ounce (3 grams) per 10x20 tray
Medium seeds: 1/2 an ounce (10-15 grams) per 10x20 tray
Big seeds: 1 ounce (25 grams) + per 10x20 tray

Using this in combination with your seed's supplier guidelines, you will be able to make an educated first guess at seeding densities. Don't forget to write down the information for later reference so you can adjust your seeding rates.

Location

Next, let's look into where you can grow your microgreens.

Kitchen

Most people who grow microgreens for fun like to grow their plants in the kitchen. When your plants are in the kitchen, they are close to the sink, making it easy to water. They are also close to where you cook so when they are done growing, you can easily cut some off and throw them on top of your dish.

The kitchen may not always be the best option to grow microgreens. This is because the plants need to get adequate sunlight. If your kitchen has good sunlight, it is a great choice. If not, you may want to choose a different location in your home.

Near a window
Another preferred place to grow microgreens is by a window. This ensures that your plants will get good light throughout the day because you are choosing the location for its light and not for its convenience. Remember that you can use a rack to make planting near a window an option if your kitchen does not have adequate light.

Any other room
If the kitchen or a windowsill is not an option, don't worry. There are many other options. Microgreens can be grown in just about any place. You can also grow microgreens on a shelf placed in any room of your house if you give it adequate artificial light.

The lights that we talked about earlier – the T5 6500K TL lights - can provide your plants with all the light they need.

Basement
Now that we have covered where to grow your microgreens regarding the main living areas of your home, let's look into some more creative areas where you could choose to grow your microgreens.

If you want to grow microgreens on a large scale inside your home but do not want it to take up all of your living space, consider turning your basement into a place for your plants. You could have many racks filled with trays of microgreens filling up the space. You will need to use artificial light to provide adequate lighting. I know many people who turned their basement to a professional grow room.

Another advantage of using your basement is that the temperature and humidity will be quite stable.

Greenhouse
If you are looking to grow your microgreens outside of your home, you could consider building a greenhouse. This is a nice option because you can make the space as big or as small as you would like it to be. It's also a space dedicated to growing your plants, so you can really focus on creating the perfect atmosphere for the optimal growth of your microgreens.

If you already have a greenhouse and you have some extra space, you can use it to grow your microgreens. A benefit of using a greenhouse is that there is no need for extra light. A disadvantage is that you can't grow through winter if you don't have heat mats available.

Growing efficiently in greenhouses is only available in the areas where the climate is adequate. You should look for a backup plan in winter once it starts to freeze. Keep an eye out for your heating bill.

Shipping container
If you are running a commercial operation from your basement or from your own home and need to expand to a larger space, a shipping container might be a great option.

You need to make sure you put it in a shady area because it can get hot quickly during midday. Once it's set up, it's a clean area and the perfect size to have a rack on each side of the container. It's also portable!

A pre-manufactured shipping container from contekpro

In your garden
You could even consider growing your microgreens in a garden
outside. However, this should not be used for commercial
growing. It's not reliable and should only be done if you are
doing it for fun.

If you are growing microgreens in your garden, make sure to
protect them against unwanted animals who like microgreens.

As you can see, there are many options as to where you can plant
your microgreens.
If you want to grow for fun, you can do it in your kitchen, by a
window or in your already existing greenhouse (if your climate
allows it). If you are growing commercially you are better off
using a separate grow room like your basement, a spare room, or
even a shipping container.

Temperature

The ideal room temperature should be around 70 degrees (21°C). The soil should be at the same temperature. Try to keep it between 60 and 80 degrees (15-26.5°C).

If the temperature drops below 60 degrees, you will experience slower growth for your microgreens.

Too much of a temperature difference during day and night-time can lead to too much stress which can interrupt the growing cycle of your microgreens.

You will have big temperature fluctuations in a greenhouse. It's important to have an exhaust fan which will bring cool air in or hot air out during the day. At night you can use heat mats or use a heater if it drops below 60°F (15°C).

Humidity

You will not only need to pay attention to the temperature of the air around your plants, but you will need to keep an eye on the humidity levels as well. It is recommended that you keep the humidity levels to 40-50 percent. If the humidity is too high it will create mold. You can use a dehumidifier to help you get the air to be at the right percentage for your plants. We talked about the dehumidifier earlier on in the advanced equipment chapter.

Watering

Let's look into watering your microgreens. To do this, you will want to use the water that you can drink. I don't recommend using any other type of water if you are not testing it first for hardness and e. Coli.

If you are soaking the seeds, the best option is to make sure you are using a pH of 6 (more details later).

Once the seeds have germinated, you need to water your microgreens from the bottom without making the leaves wet. If you make the leaves wet, they can become wilted and mold can form on the microgreens.

Tap water may have chlorine or chloramine in it. Most growers do not filter their water. If you want to filter the chloramine or chlorine use the following method:

- Chlorine can be removed by exposing it to air for a few days. When you aerate the water, the chlorine will disappear faster.

- Chloramine can't be aired out and needs to be filtered. You do this by using carbon or reverse osmosis filter.

If you are just starting out, I recommend keeping it simple by just using regular tap water. I use tap water without any problem. A lot of commercial growers don't bother with taking out chlorine and chloramine.

Tip: If your microgreens are wilting, that's a good sign that you are too late with watering them. Wilting can also occur when microgreens are sown too far from each other which makes them droop.

You can expect to use around one cup to one cup and a half per day to water your microgreens per 10x20 flat.

Soaking your seeds

Do you need to soak your seeds before planting them?
It depends.

If you have large seeds or seeds with hard pods like sunflowers or peas you should soak them. Soaking should be done in a bucket or jar (depending on the quantity). The seeds need to be submerged for 6-8 hours in a dark place with a pH of 6.

Germinating microgreens prefer a pH of 6 (more acidic) at germination which is slightly lower than municipal tap water which has a pH of 7 to 7.5. Adding 2 tablespoons of lime per gallon of water will take down the pH from 7 to 6. You can use a cheap test strip to test the pH of your water.

Again, most growers don't bother lowering their pH. In the case your germination rate is low, you can try to lower your pH and see if it helps.

Cheap pH test strips

Some small seeds become sticky when they are soaked. This a gel-like layer that develops around the seed in order to help it germinate. These are very hard to sprinkle over your grow media once they are soaked. Therefore, you do not need to soak these small seeds. Using the misting bottle on these seeds will be adequate.

Soaking is mainly used to speed up the germination process. It helps to soften the seed hull, so it takes less time for the root to penetrate the seed hull.

Germination time

Germination time is also referred to as blackout time or cover time. It's the time where the seeds establish their roots and start to sprout. To mimic the natural process of a plant, germination needs to happen in a wet and dark environment. That's why you should cover the seeds with a blackout dome so no light will reach the seeds in the first few days.

After a few days (usually 3) you will see that the plants are starting to grow. Once the stem reaches up it's time to uncover the plants and let them soak up the light. The length of the stem depends on the microgreens you would like to grow. If it's a larger microgreen like sunflower you can let the stem grow up to two inches before you uncover them.

The stem will have a yellow color at first. Once you expose them to light, they will turn green because of photosynthesis.

Weighing down seedlings

Sometimes people like to put weight on the seeds during blackout time. This is to encourage the plant to grow a strong root and stem. You can use a brick on top of another blackout tray to get it weighed down.

This technique is used for microgreens that grow high like sunflowers. The stem needs to be strong in order not to wilt.

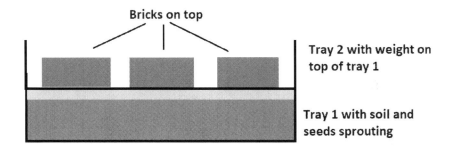

If you do this with sunflowers, they will lift the tray with the weights because of the combined force of the sprouts. When I weigh down sunflowers, I have found that the canopy stays flat (no higher or lower leaves).

Covering seeds with soil

Some growers sprinkle soil over the seeds. This is to get rid of the seed hulls (pods) of some seeds. You need to decide for yourself if you want to use this technique or not. I don't do this myself as I use a different technique to get rid of the seed hulls.

Once they are mature, I use my hand to brush over the canopy of the microgreens, this way a lot of the seed hulls will fall to the soil. When I wash the microgreens after harvesting them, the remainder of the seed hulls gets removed.

If you encounter microgreens that have their hull still attached while harvesting, try this technique.

Another method I have found that is working is to spray some water with the misting bottle on the microgreens. This will soften the remaining hulls and let them fall off the leaves easier when you use your hand to brush them.

Root hairs

Some people report that they are having mold issues from the beginning. When I ask them to take a picture and send it to me, I immediately see that it's not mold but something that's called root hairs. Root hairs develop early in the growth cycle after a seed has germinated. The hairs are there to soak up moisture and start developing the root system, so don't mistake root hairs for mold. In the following picture, you can see an example of root hairs.

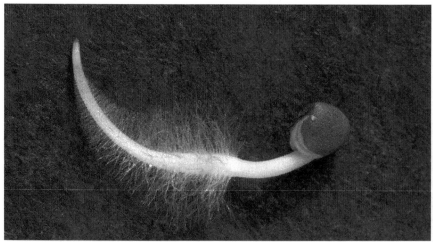

Root hairs, not to be confused with mold

Anti-mold spray

If you can't get rid of mold while limiting humidity to 40-50% and temperature to 70°F and supplying indirect air movement you only have one option left. That's to use an anti-mold spray. This should only be used as a last resort in order to save a crop.

Get yourself a regular misting bottle with a mixture of white vinegar, 3% food grade hydrogen peroxide and water in the following ratio:

- 1 part of white vinegar (50ml)
- 1 part of 3% food grade hydrogen peroxide (50ml)
- 18 parts of water (900ml)

Microgreen Varieties

In this chapter, I will give you guidelines for the most commonly grown microgreens: whether you need to soak them or not, the cover time (blackout time) and how long you can expect to wait to harvest your crop. The time can vary from person to person so don't take this as a rule, rather as a guideline. Use your own notes and experience as a reference.

Arugula
Soak: No
Cover time: 1-3 days
Time to harvest: 8-12 days
Notes: Short microgreens, around 1 ½ to 2 inches high. Tastes spicy and bitter. Also called rocket salad in other parts of the world.

Sunflower
Soak: Yes
Cover time: 2-4 days
Time to harvest: 8-14 days
Notes: Soak the seed in water that's pH balanced to 6 for 6-8 hours before seeding. Once seeded, weigh it down with another grow tray or and some weight in order for the stems to develop. Once it pushes up the weighted grow tray 2 inches, remove it and expose it to sunlight.

Kale
Soak: No
Cover time: 2-4 days
Time to harvest: 6-10 days

Radish
Soak: No
Cover time: 1-2 days
Time to harvest: 8-10 days
Notes: Fast-growing crop, tastes spicy.

Broccoli
Soak: No
Cover time: 2-3 days
Time to harvest: 6-10 days
Notes: Delicate microgreen. If you wait too long to harvest it will start to fall over.

Mustard
Soak: No
Cover time: 2-4 days
Time to harvest: 6-10 days
Notes: Spicy microgreens

Pak Choy or Bok Choy
Soak: No
Cover time: 2-3 days
Time to harvest: 8-14 days

Komatsuna
Soak: No
Cover time: 2 days
Time to harvest: 8-12 days

Cress
Soak: No
Cover time: 2 days
Time to harvest: 7-14 days
Notes: Do not soak the seeds. the seeds will develop a sticky outer shell that will bunch together. Harvest on time before they start to fall over.

Lettuce
Soak: No
Cover time: 3-4 days
Time to harvest: 8-12 days

Red-Veined Sorrel
Soak: No
Cover time: 5-8 days
Time to harvest: 21-30 days

Amaranth
Soak: No
Cover time: 3-6 days
Time to harvest: 8-14 days

Wheatgrass

Soak: Yes

Cover time: 2 days

Time to harvest: 8-10 days

Notes: Wheatgrass is used for juicing and animal feed during winter. When it's grown in large quantities it's grown using hydroponics without fertilizer. You can use the traditional method (soil) for smaller quantities. These regrow after you have cut them

Pea

Soak: Yes

Cover time: 3-5 days

Time to harvest: 8-14 days

Notes: Pea seeds have a hard shell so they take a long time to germinate. To speed it up, you should soak them first for 6-8 hours in water with a pH of 6. You can add weight on top while germinating but you don't need to (experiment with this). They can grow up to 5 inches tall.

Beet

Soak: Yes

Cover time: 6-8 days

Time to harvest: 10-14 days

Notes: The hulls of the beets are not easy to get rid of. Brush the canopy with your hands to get rid of the seed hulls. It might be a good option to cover the seeds with a half-inch of soil first to get rid of the seed hulls.

Swiss Chard
Soak: Yes
Cover time: 4-7 days
Time to harvest: 10-14 days
Notes: Each seedpod contains 4-5 seeds. Don't expose them to light too soon and give them enough space. Not an easy one to grow. If this crop fails, try to cover them with a half-inch of soil to make them germinate better.

Cilantro
Soak: No
Cover time: 6-7 days
Time to harvest: 18-23 days
Notes: Try to order split seeds because each seed pod has two seeds in it. Some people soak them. If your harvest fails, try to soak them to improve germination.

Basil
Soak: No
Cover time: 4-7 days
Time to harvest: 10-15 days

Dill
Soak: No
Cover time: 2-4 days
Time to harvest: 15-20 days

Buckwheat
Soak: Yes
Cover time: 3-4 days
Time to harvest: 8-12 days

Cabbage
Soak: No
Cover time: 2-4 days
Time to harvest: 8-12 days

Kohlrabi
Soak: No
Cover time: 2-4 days
Time to harvest: 10-14 days

Celery
Soak: No
Cover time: 6-8 days
Time to harvest: 18-22 days

Leek
Soak: No
Cover time: 3-5 days
Time to harvest: 12-14 days

Fennel
Soak: No
Cover time: 3-5 days
Time to harvest: 15-17 days

Step by Step Process

By the end of this chapter, you will have all the knowledge that you need to grow microgreens with ease.

Fill your tray with the growing media you have chosen. If you are using soil, you need to use one to one and a half inches of soil. Make sure there are no large particles in the soil. You can avoid this by using a screen.

I use a big empty container and put a wire screen over it. I then open my bag of germinating mix on top of the screen and push it through to break up the soil. Next, I take a 10x20 tray and put it inside a big bin to fill it up with soil using my hands. I do this with however many trays I need and then proceed to the next step.

You can press down the soil lightly in order to level out the soil. The reason you should level out the soil is so there will be no water pockets in the tray. I use a wooden board the size of the tray and press it down lightly. Don't compact it too much because it will be harder for the roots to go into the soil.

Next, you will need to moisten your soil. Use a spray bottle or a garden hose with a sprayer at the end. Make sure it drains properly and no puddles are present. Then take your seeds and sprinkle them evenly on the tray. You don't need to bury them in the soil.

Note: if you have seeds that need to be pre-soaked you should have soaked them for 6-8 hours before starting to seed.

Once you have spread the seeds you need to mist them one more time before covering them with a blackout dome. You can put a seeding tray without holes over it and cover them that way.

If you are growing sunflower microgreens you need to weigh them down using a seed tray and a brick. That way they develop strong stems.

The blackout dome has two purposes:

- To keep the light out
- To keep the moisture level high during germination

Check daily how moist the soil is and mist the microgreens if necessary. If the blackout dome has moisture on the sides and top you are doing a good job. You want the soil to be moist (especially in germination time).

Once you see that the stem is coming up, it's time to remove the germination dome and let the plants soak up the sun or artificial light you have installed. The time until uncovering depends on the kind of microgreen you are seeding. If you are seeding peas or sunflowers you can wait until they are one to two inches high before you uncover them so they will grow taller.

If you are seeding broccoli microgreens you can uncover them when they reach around a half-inch because they will not grow very tall.

Check daily if watering is necessary. Don't use the spray bottle for watering after the germination stage. It's best to water the soil directly (from the bottom) without misting the leaves and stem. This is to reduce the risk of mold growth. The soil should be kept moist, not wet.

You can either water them directly on the soil and let the excess drain to your drip tray or you can pour water in the drip tray for the roots to soak it up from there. Don't worry, the roots will have extended to the bottom of the tray after germination.

Next, let's look into what your plant should look like when they are ready to harvest. Luckily, you should be able to tell by looking at your plant that it will be ready to be harvested soon. This will help you to be prepared and to know when the time is right as well. Microgreens can either be harvested during the cotyledon stage (first two leaves or seed leaves) or they can be harvested during the true leaf stage.

The cotyledon is also considered the embryonic leaf of a plant. The cotyledon stage is when the plant sprouts out of the ground and the first two leaves appear. This is the stage that tastes the best for most types of microgreens.

The true leaf stage is when the plant has already passed its cotyledon stage. As you can guess from the name, the true leaf stage is when the plant gets its first set of true leaves. Microgreens that are more bitter in flavor are best when they are harvested during this stage. An example of a type of plant that would taste best eaten in the true leaf stage as a microgreen would be any type of lettuce.

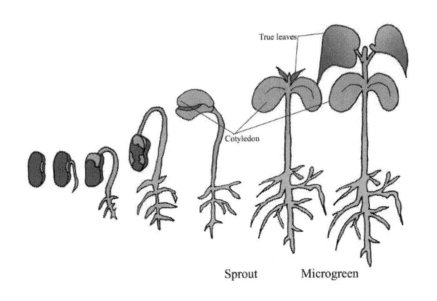

True leaves

Cotyledon

Sprout   Microgreen

Development into the microgreen stage
Image from sciencedirect.com

Once you know that your microgreens are ready, it will be time to do the actual harvesting. To do this, you will need a knife or scissors depending on which tool allows you to be the most comfortable while you are cutting your microgreens. You will want the scissors or knife to be sharp so that it is able to cut through the stems of your plants easily and smoothly.

You will want to cut the stems of your plants just above the soil line. The height of the plants when you cut them will depend on how big they grew in the short time since they sprouted. Typically, you will find yourself cutting the stems of the plants between half of an inch to one inch above the soil.

Another good tip to remember when you are choosing when to harvest your plants is that you can taste a small amount of your microgreens before you harvest them. When you taste them, consider writing in a journal about how they tasted and how many days or weeks it has been since you have sown them. If you do this, you will be able to pinpoint the perfect time to harvest your microgreens.

The perfect time to harvest microgreens is not a magic number that you can find in a book or on the internet, because it is a different answer for every person. This is because everyone who grows microgreens uses different growing systems, techniques, and locations. These are the things that make your microgreens grow either quickly or slowly.

The next stage is cleaning them. If you don't want to clean them or there is no contamination of the soil or seed hulls you can just harvest them and put them in your food. However, when you are selling them, I recommend giving them a wash first.

When you harvest your microgreens, it is extremely important that you clean your crop as soon as possible.

In order to wash your microgreens, you will want to rinse them in cold water before enjoying them with your salads or in your smoothies. You could also choose to fill your clean kitchen sink with cold water to soak the microgreens before you eat them as this provides a thorough clean to ensure there is no soil left.

If you leave them wet and store them for later use, they will quickly begin to go bad in the fridge. Because of this, you need to always remember to dry your microgreens after you go through the process of cleaning them.

To dry your microgreens, you will benefit greatly from owning a salad spinner. If you use the salad spinner in combination with some paper towels, you will be able to get just about all of the water off of your crop.

Another option to dry them is to spread them out on a screen (where air can freely flow under and on top). A herb dryer is perfect for this purpose. You can use a fan to speed up the drying process. This is the most passive method but takes the longest amount of time.

Next, you should get rid of the soil you used to grow your microgreens. You can throw it on the composting pile for later use in the garden. Some people reuse their soil once it has composted. I do not recommend doing this because there could be harmful bacteria and could create mold outbreaks.

You not only need to be careful about bacteria growing on your crop, but you need to look out for these dangerous bacteria on your growing materials as well. One of the items that you should clean to ensure that there are no bacteria is your growing trays.

In order to clean your growing trays, you should start by emptying the soil. Next, rinse your tray with clean water. If necessary, scrub the dirt of the trays.

Remember that rinsing with water only removes the remainder of the debris and it is not enough to ensure that the tray is free from harmful germs.

To make sure these dangerous germs go away for good, you should soak your trays in a bleach solution after each growing cycle. Bleach is the only way to fully ensure that all those bacteria are gone for good.

Use one tablespoon of bleach for every gallon of water. This is by far the easiest method. Soak them for a few minutes and make sure the water and bleach solution makes contact with all the trays.

Some people use different methods to clean their trays, but you do need to know that these methods are not as safe as simply doing a bleach soak. Some people choose to clean their trays with hydrogen peroxide.

A simple bleach soak is the easiest option to ensure a complete clean. This is the only cleaning option that I would recommend for you to use.

The last thing on the to-do list is to clean your harvesting area to make it ready for another batch of seedlings.

Troubleshooting

Microgreens are falling over

Check your seeding density. Microgreens falling over means they are not sown dense enough. Increase the density so the microgreens can 'rest' on each other. That's why it's good practice to keep a notebook and write down your seed densities.

Microgreens falling over

Mold on microgreens

Mold on microgreens is a common problem. To avoid mold on your microgreens, check the following parameters which will reduce mold forming:

- Water from the bottom:
  After germination, always water your plants from the bottom. Water on the leaves creates a very damp environment which they really don't need. It's better to water your microgreens from the bottom or water into the corner of the tray. Using this method, the water will be directly absorbed by the roots, where it's needed.

- Make sure there is enough airflow:
  If you don't have enough airflow, the water that's evaporated from the potting mix is trapped under the foliage. Increasing airflow in the room will remove the dampness between the potting mix and the leaves. Don't point a fan directly at the microgreens because it can dry out the soil.

- Check for proper humidity levels:
  Again, if the air in your grow room is too humid, mold will form. Keep an eye on the humidity level. Aim for around 40-50% humidity. A dehumidifier or a humidifier can help you reach those levels. If you can't control humidity, your best option is to improve the airflow.

- Don't reuse your potting mix:
  Reusing your potting mix is a big no-no. The roots of the previous harvest will still be present in the soil and mold can grow on them. Play it safe and always use a sterile potting mix.

When watering microgreens, you need them to be moist, not flooded or very wet. When you are getting more experienced you can check if your microgreens need water by holding and guessing the weight of the tray. If the tray is light, you need to water them. If the tray is heavy, they probably don't need any water. Don't expect to develop this gift from the beginning, this comes with experience.

When you start it's a good idea to have a drip tray underneath your microgreen tray. The excess water from the microgreens can drip through resulting in a wet but not soaked potting mix. After practicing you will know precisely how much water you need to give your microgreens.

Stems are too short

If you feel like your stems are shorter than normal, you should extend the germination time. You can extend the germination time using a blackout dome to cover the microgreens. When seeds sprout, they want to reach up for light, thus growing in length. When you uncover them too quickly, the microgreen doesn't have any reason to put its energy into growing vertically. Instead, it will begin to develop leaves.

If you leave the cover on, the plant thinks it's still under the soil. It will grow taller until the blackout dome is removed. At this point, the plant thinks it's above the soil and starts to develop its leaves. You should uncover most microgreens when they reach around 1 ½ inch tall.

Too many seed hulls on top

Seed hulls don't taste great. That's why you want to get rid of them. The first method I will recommend is brushing them off with your hands. This will remove most of the seed hulls.

It could be you are harvesting too early. The seed hulls normally fall off after the cotyledon stage. If you harvest before that stage, there are still many hulls present. Wait until the true leaves appear.

It helps to soak the seeds for germination. Soaking the seeds makes the hull softer which will make it easier for the microgreen to get rid of it.

Washing them and soaking the seeds in water will let the hulls float to the surface. You can then take the seed hulls out of the water and let your microgreens dry.

If you can't get rid of the hulls using the previous methods, consider covering your seeds with a bit of soil mix. When the seeds germinate, they have to push themselves through about ½ inch of potting mix in order to reach the light. The process of the sprout going through the potting mix will result in the seed hulls falling off.

Microgreens taste bitter

If your microgreens taste bitter, it's a sign that you need to wait longer or have waited too long to harvest them. Taste them every day so you know when they are at their best. Note down the day when they tasted their best. Most microgreens are harvested right after the first true leaves appear.

Harvesting microgreens without soil

When harvesting your microgreens, you might end up with some soil on your microgreens. A good method to counter having soil in your microgreens is to keep your cutting tool level with the tray.

For example, take your scissors and hold them horizontally to the tray. Don't use the scissors at an angle because the tip of the scissors might dig itself through the soil which will result in a harvest of microgreens and some soil.

Grab the top of the microgreens with your hand and cut them. You might want to consider using a one-inch high tray so you can easily cut them at the base of their stem.

If you cut horizontally and not downward, your microgreens will have more stems. If you get more stems, they will weigh more which will benefit you if you are growing commercially and sell by weight.

If you have inexpensive soil and use a 2-inch high tray, you can use a bit more soil to raise the microgreens to a point where they are easier to cut.

Microgreen Recipes

Now that we have learned all about what microgreens are and how to grow and harvest them in an efficient and safe manner, let's look into how we can use microgreens. As we mentioned earlier in the book, microgreens are commonly used in salads, soups, and smoothies. In this chapter, we will look at some recipes that use microgreens.

Smoothies

First, let's look at a microgreens smoothie recipe that chocolate lovers will not be able to get enough of. This recipe is called Chocolate Superfood Smoothie.

You will need:

- One whole banana
- Three-fourths of a cup of chocolate-flavored almond milk
- One Tbsp of almond butter
- Between one and three tsp of cocoa powder
- One handful of microgreens of your choosing (Kale is a good option for this)
- One half of a cup of ice
- Cinnamon to taste

To make this smoothie, you will want to put all of these ingredients into a blender and then blend until the drink is smooth in texture.

Let's look at a fruitier option for a microgreen smoothie next. This recipe is called Tropical Superfood Smoothie.
You will need:

- One whole banana
- One half of a cup of pineapple juice (fresh or canned)
- One half of a cup of coconut milk, unsweetened
- One or two tbsp of shredded coconut flesh
- One cup of ice
- One handful of microgreens (Broccoli is a good choice here)

To make this smoothie you will again put all the ingredients into a blender and then blend them together until they are smooth in texture.

Salads
Now that we have looked into smoothies, let's move on to salads. If you enjoy the flavor of your microgreens, you will love to have them mixed into a good salad recipe so that you are able to enjoy their flavors to the fullest.

First, let's look at a recipe for a homemade microgreen salad.
You will need:

- One cup of your favorite microgreens
- One half of an avocado cut into cubes
- One half of a carrot, shredded
- One orange, cut into cubes
- One-fourth of a cup of walnuts
- One tablespoon of cold-pressed olive oil
- One tablespoon of lemon juice
- One clove of garlic, chopped
- Salt and pepper to taste

To make this salad, you will want to ensure that all your ingredients are clean.

Chop the avocado and orange into cubes and shred the carrot. You will then dump these ingredients into a bowl with your microgreens and your walnuts.

Next, you will want to make your dressing. In this recipe, the dressing is a type of vinaigrette. Make this by combining your olive oil, lemon juice, garlic, salt and pepper in a separate bowl. You can then top your salad with your vinaigrette dressing and enjoy.

Let's look at another microgreen salad recipe. This recipe is called Microgreen Lime Salad.

The salad includes:

- One cup of your favorite microgreens
- Six chopped or sliced radishes
- One-eighth of a teaspoon of mustard powder
- One-fourth of a teaspoon of salt
- Four tablespoons of olive oil
- Two tablespoons of lime juice
- Salt and pepper to taste

To make this salad, you will want to first make sure that your ingredients are clean and ready to go. You can chop or slice your radishes and place them in a bowl. You will then take the rest of the ingredients and stir them together. This will make the dressing for your salad. When the dressing is made, you can pour it on top of your microgreen and radish mixture to enjoy as a salad.

Soups

Now that we have looked into salads, let's look at another way to enjoy microgreens. If you are looking for a unique way to incorporate microgreens into your food or if you do not like the flavor of raw microgreens, you could consider putting them in your favorite soup.

Let's look at some microgreens soup recipes now. The first recipe is called Microgreen Broccoli Soup.

You will need:

- One whole head of broccoli cut into pieces
- One yellow onion cut into wedges
- Four cloves of garlic peeled and left whole
- Two cups of broccoli microgreens
- Four cups of vegetable broth
- One cup of navy beans (These can be from a can or cooked by you)
- One tablespoon of grapeseed oil
- One-fourth of a teaspoon of salt
- The juice of half a lemon
- One half of a teaspoon of chili powder
- Two tablespoons of olive oil
- Three tablespoons of sunflower seeds, not salted and preferably roasted
- Three ounces of chopped feta cheese

To make this recipe, you can start by cooking the broccoli in the oven with the garlic and onion, sprinkled with the salt and olive oil. Set the oven to 425 degrees and cook for 25 minutes. You can stir the food on the tray halfway through to help it cook more evenly as well.

Next, put your vegetable broth in a big pot on top of the stove, then add your roasted broccoli, garlic, and onions. You will then want to put your navy beans, feta cheese, microgreens, lemon juice, and chili powder in a blender or food processor.

Blend these ingredients together until they are smooth in texture then add this mixture into your pot of soup.

With these recipes, you should have a good start on how you can enjoy your microgreens in your kitchen. These recipes also wrap up our section on how to grow microgreens for fun. In this section, you probably have gone from knowing not much at all about microgreens to knowing exactly what they are, as well as how to grow them and how to use them.

In the next section of the book, we will look into how to grow microgreens for a profit instead of only growing them for yourself.

Growing Microgreens Commercially

Before You Begin Your Venture

So now that we know all about how you can enjoy microgreens on your own, let's look into how you can grow them commercially. Before you begin to grow microgreens at home and sell them for a profit, there are a few things that you need to know. In this chapter, we will get you ready to start your journey in the microgreens business by looking into food safety, government rules for selling microgreens, market research, and how you can become a certified organic grower.

First, we will talk about food safety. In the previous section of the book, we looked into how to keep your plants clean before you eat them. When you sell your microgreens, you need to have a good cleaning process because the stakes are higher. Of course you do not want to make yourself, your friends, or family sick with the microgreens that you grow in your kitchen windowsill.

However, it is a much bigger deal if you sell microgreens to many people whom you do not even know if they end up getting sick from eating the microgreens you produce.

One simple thing that you will need to be very aware of when you are growing microgreens with the end goal of selling them commercially is washing your hands. You will need to wash your hands every single time that you touch your microgreens.

To make sure that you are washing your hands well enough, you may want to go back to the handwashing styles that you probably remember learning in elementary school. You need to use warm water and soap. Here are the steps in case you forgot:

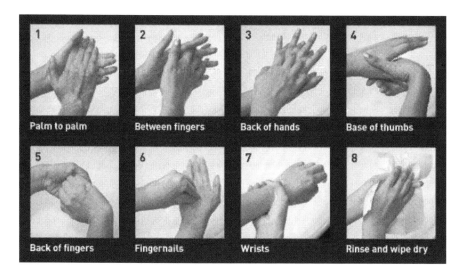

Seeds can also be contaminated before you plant them. To avoid this, make sure that you are buying your seeds from a good and trustworthy source. You could even call the seed company to ask them what they do to avoid contamination of their seeds.

Next, let's investigate what the government has to say about the safety of selling microgreens in the USA. The government does have some rules to make sure that microgreens that are sold for a profit are grown in a safe and healthy way. The FDA oversees the safety of the foods that are sold in the United States. Because of this, you will want to follow the rules that the FDA enforces when you sell your crop so that you are able to ensure that it is completely safe.

The FDA is combining the rules for sprouts together with microgreens. Make sure you read the following pdf on their website to comply with the rules:

https://www.fda.gov/media/102430/download

The first thing that the FDA wants to ensure is that you are using water that is safe. Their first requirement for your product to be labeled safe by the FDA is labeled as "water quality".

To determine water quality, you need to make sure that there is no E. coli present in your water. E. Coli can be found in well water or standing water. If you are using tap water, you don't have to worry about this.

The second thing that the FDA requires has to do with the growing media that you choose to use. If you choose to use manure in your soil, you need to wait for 4 months before you can actually plant your seeds in the soil to make sure that there are no bacteria that will enter and contaminate your microgreens

Compost should not be used to grow microgreens commercially

The next two requirements that the FDA has for produce have to do with sprouts and produce that is near grazing animals Neither of these has anything to do with microgreens. The grazing animals' rule does not apply because you cannot have grazing animals together with your microgreens.

The fifth rule the FDA has about growing produce has to do with worker training. If you have people who work for you to help you sell your microgreens, this will apply to you. You will need to make sure that your workers are fully trained on how to safely care for the plants in order to avoid the spreading of bacteria. For example, they must be trained on how to wash their hands well before they touch the crops and after they touch the crops.

The sixth and final rule that the FDA has regarding selling produce is about equipment. The equipment you use, whether it's a microgreens harvester or just the greenhouse structure that you grow inside of, needs to be properly cleaned. This once again helps to avoid contamination of the microgreens. In some big commercial systems, you can see that people have to sanitize (remove bacteria) their shoes before they enter.

If you follow these rules put out by the FDA about produce, you should be able to sell the microgreens that you grow. These rules will help you to make sure that your plants are not contaminated and that they are safe for people to eat.

Market research

Next, let's look into doing some market research on microgreens. Is there really a demand for microgreens in your area? Luckily, microgreens are popular in healthy eating right now so there is quite a large demand in general.

To figure out if there is a demand in your area, you may want to consider visiting all of the local markets in your area. Are there people there who are selling microgreens? If there are a few different booths at each market that has microgreens for sale, the demand is quite high, but the market could be saturated.

This is because there are already people near you who are selling the same thing. However, if you went to all of the markets and only saw one microgreen stand in one location with a long line of customers near it, the demand for microgreens in your area is probably high while competition is low.

The next thing you need to do is figuring out your cost per ounce of microgreens. You do this by growing them and adding up all the expenses. Next, you compare this number with what you find at the supermarket or organic market. Can you compete with this price if you must pay your bills and make a living?

Why should people buy from you instead of another seller? Do not compete only on price but also on quality. You need to differentiate yourself from your competition.

I will talk more about places to sell your microgreens later. Different places will have different pricing.

Becoming certified organic

Something else that will help with more demand is growing your microgreens organically. Organic foods are very popular in our culture today, especially to people who are health conscious.

These health-conscious people who buy organic foods are probably the same people who care enough about their health to learn about things like microgreens and who eventually decide to purchase and consume them. One way to show these people that you are growing organically is by becoming something that is called "certified organic".

The first thing that you need to do to become certified organic is to look online and choose a certifier who is USDA-accredited. This is important because if you choose someone to check over your growing techniques and they are not USDA-accredited, you will not become certified organic based on their findings even if you truly are doing everything the right way.

When you find a certified agent, you will send them an application and the fee for the application in the mail. The cost of these fees depends on two factors; the certifying agent that you choose and the size of your microgreens farm. Certain certifying agents charge more for applications than others. Likewise, different size farms cost more than others as well. The cost of a certified organic label will cost you $200-$1500 including application fee, site inspection fee, and yearly license fee.

Typically, the larger the farm is, the more the application will cost you. Because of this, it may be a good idea to become certified organic while your farm is still small. You can always expand later, but this will help you get certified for a little bit less of a fee in the meantime.

Once the certifying agent receives your application and your fee, they will look over your application. They will read all the details that you send in to ensure that you really are growing your microgreens to the standards that they are looking for.

Of course, you will want to make sure that you really are following the standards. To start that process, you need to at least know the standards. The USDA's agricultural marketing service has a great interactive video to show you exactly how to start making your farm organic if you would like a visual place to start learning. We will also cover the information here as well.

The Certification Process

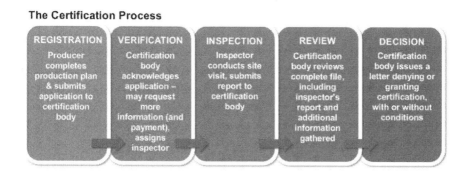

REGISTRATION	VERIFICATION	INSPECTION	REVIEW	DECISION
Producer completes production plan & submits application to certification body	Certification body acknowledges application – may request more information (and payment), assigns inspector	Inspector conducts site visit, submits report to certification body	Certification body reviews complete file, including inspector's report and additional information gathered	Certification body issues a letter denying or granting certification, with or without conditions

For more information watch this video:

https://practicalgrowing.com/become-organic

The two most important items on your list should be using non-GMO seeds and no pesticides. For more information on how to become Certified Organic I recommend visiting the USDA official website because these rules can and will always change:

https://www.usda.gov/topics/organic

After you ensure that your microgreen farm is being grown organically and the certifying agent approves your application, they will make a visit to your location. They will come to your site to look around and make sure that everything that you said on your application was true. If you truly are following the guidelines in order to be organic, this visit should not be a problem at all. However, if your agent shows up and finds you spraying weeds with a jug of Roundup your visit will definitely not go as well as you want it to.

The agent will go back to their office and look at the details of the visit alongside your application. This is when they officially decide whether your farm follows the USDA rules in order for it to be labeled as "certified organic". This is the final decision in your application process.

After the final decision is made, your certifying agent will reach out to you with an answer. If you did not pass, your agent will let you know why, and your application will be dismissed.

If you meet all the guidelines according to the certifying agent, they will issue you a certificate that states that you are certified organic. You can then use this label in your marketing campaigns to show people that your product truly is organic. This is a label that people know they can trust, so it will greatly benefit the demand of your produce.

Seed testing

Another important thing that you need to do when you are growing your microgreens is to make sure that your seeds are of high quality. You can purchase seeds with a good reputation, but you may want to do your own testing to ensure that the seeds are working well for you. One way to do this is through germination testing. It may seem like a lot of work, but it will be worth it to make sure that the seeds are of good quality.

To do germination testing, take a small growing container and 20 seeds. Then let them germinate and see how many of the seeds are developing into microgreens. If you know how many seeds you put in and how many started to grow you know your germination rate.

For example, I started with 20 seeds and I see 17 seeds that have germinated. The germination rate is (17*5) 85%. If your germination rate is below 80% you are losing 20% of your seeds which will be costly. Test other seed companies or refine your growing method to increase germination rates.

Packaging

Another thing that you will need to pay attention to when selling your microgreens is packaging. The packaging is a big part of marketing these days. If you have an attractive package, it could set you apart from the competition even if your product is the same quality. Because of this, it is something that you really need to think about when you are selling your product. One option that you could use is compostable containers. This makes your business have less of an environmental impact, which customers will notice.

At the same time, it also makes people more interested in buying your product because it helps to reduce their environmental footprint. It is also a way to show your customers that you are a business worth supporting because your morals are in the right place.

If compostable containers are not something that you are interested in or are not something that is in your budget, you could consider plastic bags or hard plastic boxes. Plastic bags are easy to come by and they are commonly used. Hard plastic boxes are able to protect your microgreens in a variety of circumstances. They will protect them from not getting smashed underneath things while you travel with your product.

Keep in mind though, that many people are moving away from using plastic for containers because of the environmental impact that it causes. A lot of people that buy organic also care about the environment. Because of this, if you want people to buy your organic microgreens, you might want to consider using environmentally friendly packaging to encourage people to buy your product over other products.

You could consider using cardboard boxes or foldable plastic crates to deliver your microgreens to chefs. Cardboard boxes are cheap, and they are easy to come by. They also protect your microgreens pretty well. Cardboard boxes are recyclable. This makes them a little bit more attractive to environmentally friendly customers than single-use plastic bags.

Foldable plastic crate for restaurants

Another option is a heat-sealed plastic bag. They don't need as much plastic but are very fragile.

The most used packaging for microgreens is the 16 oz plastic clamshell box. It will hold around 2 oz of microgreens. It's the most used one because it's cheap, and it protects your delicate microgreens. You can use a label on top to tell customers more about your product.

Most used package for microgreens: the 16oz clamshell

Labeling

Aside from the actual package that you put your product in, you also need to think about labels. You may want to have a professional help you to design a logo to represent your business. You could put this on the label for your microgreens to show people where their product came from.

This is a good marketing technique because if people see your label, they may want to find out more about your business and support it if they like your product. You also want your labels to be clear and concise, so people know what they are buying.

Consider looking at labels of other products like yours. This can help you figure out what you would like your labels to look like

You can figure out what is successful on a label and what is not successful based on what other people choose to use and how their businesses are going. This is what you should consider printing on your label:

- Your logo
- Type of microgreen
- Date of harvest
- If you are approved for USDA organic, put it on there
- Non-GMO if that's the case

You may also want to consider purchasing a heat sealer. This is only important if you choose to package your product in transparent plastic bags. If you have a heat sealer, you can seal your package so that it is able to stay fresher longer.

You may also want to consider live microgreens packaging. Live packaging means that the microgreen is still in the growing media. The roots can still soak up some water to stay fresh.

You can put the growing medium at the bottom and let the plants continue to stay alive while they are contained. This helps to make your plants last longer when people buy them. It is also an attractive marketing tool because people think that it is unique, and they know that they are getting a fresh product if they buy microgreens in that style.

Chefs will accept both cut and live microgreens, but they do not like soil in their kitchen. Therefore, bio felt is a better option if chefs want to use your live microgreens.

Pricing

According to a study, total input costs are around $2.46/ft^2$ and the yield is 1.5 ounces/ft^2 to 4 ounces/ft^2 depending on the variety. Market prices vary from $2 to $6 per ounce. Which leaves you with a margin of 35% to 75%.

Study: Bachman, Gary & Coker, Christine. (2013). Economics of Growing Microgreens for the Local Food Market, Poster Board #064

Follow this link to read a market research analysis for a microgreens farm:

- **https://practicalgrowing.com/microgreens-case-study**

You need to make sure that you are at least going to make a profit and you need to decide how much profit you would like to make. Also, you should consider making this choice based on how much other people are charging for their microgreens.
You do not want to be too far above this price point because people will never buy your product if it is more expensive for the same thing. You also don't want to be too much below this price point, because if you are too far under the market price, you may not make as much of a profit as you can.

If you are selling your microgreens in a place other than the farm you will have to figure out transportation. You need to be able to refrigerate your microgreens while you are transporting them. You can use a refrigeration box with ice for this.

As we mentioned earlier, when you were figuring out how much to charge for your microgreens, you need to figure out how much you have already spent in order to see if you could make a profit. There are many costs involved in growing microgreens. One of the costs is the initial investment of the system that you use for growing. You will also need to take into account the following costs:

- Original investment spread over a few years
- Seeds (depending on variety)
- Soil (around $1 per 10x20 flat)
- Packaging ($0.10)
- Labels ($0.05)
- Electricity cost ($0.3)
- Water cost (negligible)
- Marketing cost
- Insurance cost
- Rent
- Storage
- Bookkeeping
- Labor
- Transportation to market or grocery store

You will also want to look into how much time you spend growing your plants, to ensure that your labor is paid for. If you are not paid for how much you are working, you probably will not be able to continue to do your business for long. You need to make enough money to cover your business cost but also to cover how much you are working.

If your costs are too high because you must cover all these things, you might have to figure out how to cut costs or find a more efficient way. You could look into buying your seeds and grow media in bulk. You could also look into how much you are spending on your electrical bill and see if there is any way that you could use less power or use natural lighting.

Overall, there are a lot of things that you need to look at when you choose to sell your microgreens. If you use this list from this chapter to figure out what you need to look into, you should be able to make a good profit from your microgreens if your location allows it.

Marketing and Sales

Now that we have learned how to grow your microgreens for a profit and how to get them ready to sell, let's figure out how we can find people to buy your microgreens.

Starting a successful business is hard.
Finding reliable customers will be harder.

If you have a good marketing strategy and a good plan for sales, this struggle can be avoided.

In this chapter, you will learn all the about marketing and sales of microgreens and I will do my best to provide you with ways in which you can be successful while selling your microgreens on your own.

I highly recommend creating a brand for your business and sharing your progress on social media (more on this later). For example, 'Brad's Microgreens'.

Here are some ways you can market your microgreens to different customers.

Schools

First, we are going to start looking at different ways that you can sell microgreens in specific places. One place that you may want to start selling your microgreens is on a college campus or university kitchen. Healthy student meals become more important now and get a lot more attention. Be prepared to reduce your price because you are selling in bulk.

Hospitals

Another place that might be a good location to sell your microgreens to are private owned hospitals. These hospitals go the extra mile for their customers and might want to include some fresh microgreens in their meals. Always try to speak to the chef instead of the head of the hospital. Deliver some samples or cold call the person that's planning the meals.

Restaurants

Selling to different restaurants might be your biggest source of income. They produce consistent sales. You can grow your microgreens according to the order you have from the chef. Outreach to chefs in your neighborhood is crucial for your business plan. Try to give the chef free samples and come back the next week and ask how they were and if they would like to place an order. If not, offer them some different microgreens. Persistence is key here. Only offer them the best quality microgreens.

Offer them the two options of delivery, live or cut microgreens. Give them a sheet with all your information and possible microgreens you can grow. You can also cold call restaurants.

Retail stores

Retail may be a good option for a place to sell your microgreens as well. You could approach health food stores and ask them if they have space for your product on the shelves. To do this, you would need to offer a portion of your proceeds to the store.

However, this still would benefit you greatly because it would allow your product to be sold with little work at your end. It would also allow your product to be seen by more people which will increase the number of customers that you have. To partner with a health food store, you could call them and ask them if they take partnerships or you could go into the store and offer the owner some samples of your microgreens together with a list of your produce.

The latter of these options is more personal and may be a better choice. If you are very friendly and offer a great product, the store may be more likely to allow you to sell their product on their shelves.

Farmers Markets

Selling at farmers' markets is also a good opportunity. Not only to sell your microgreens to customers but to network with other sellers and maybe even trade some of your microgreens for other produce.

Having a network of people doing the same thing as you will result in more knowledge and introductions to future business sales.

For example, the stand next to you sells mushrooms to restaurants. He might introduce you to the restaurant chef and let them know you are selling quality microgreens. This connection might lead to further business opportunities.

You can get into the juicing trend. Wheatgrass is a popular microgreen people use to juice. Simply take a cold press juicer and put wheatgrass in the hopper, then turn manually or use electricity to produce a healthy juice. I'm sure many people will stop by to get a shot!

Cold press juicer

Online

As you are aware, many things today are being purchased on the Internet and not in person. Because of this, you could consider selling them online.

A good option on how to do this would be to set up a monthly/weekly subscription service so that you are growing the same number of microgreens every month or week. This way, you will have buyers for these greens no matter what. When you have people sign up to purchase your product, you will always know how much microgreens you need to grow.

Social Media Marketing

People like to spend time on sites like Facebook and Instagram. They use the sites to connect with their friends, but they also can see new products being advertised.

If you share pictures of the growing process or why you are doing what you are doing, it may help people to feel more of a personal connection to your business. If people feel a more personal connection to your business, they may be more likely to buy from you than from someone else whom they don't know at all.

Even if you do not actually know these people in real life, social media can help them feel like they know your brand which can then allow them to buy more from you than they would otherwise.

The greatest potential of social media marketing is that you can run advertisements to people who are interested in healthy living and live near the area you are in. This is a very powerful marketing opportunity as many microgreen growers don't bother with social media marketing. You can sell recurring subscription boxes from a social media platform.

Make your own website

Making a website yourself is very easy nowadays. You can easily make one with WordPress or Shopify. This website could be filled with information that can help your clients and customers with what they are looking for. They can place orders from this website, or it could just be a website that informs them about your business.

This allows your website to pop up in Google searches when someone is looking to buy microgreens which can help you to gain new customers as well. Owning a proper website will cost you around $12 for the domain name/year and $60 in hosting for a year. Look for some tutorials on the internet about making your own website with WordPress, it's pretty easy!

Another thing that you need to know about marketing and sales is how to track your business.

If you are not able to check the sales of your business, you will not know how well your business is doing. It will be difficult for you to understand what types of profit you are making when you do not know how much you are actually making at all.

Tracking your sales can be very useful regarding which microgreen or client made you the most amount of profit.

It can help you to understand your busy season and your low season. It can also help you to understand which locations are bringing in the most revenue. Knowing this, you can make planned vacations or put more energy into the most profitable sources of income.

First, you should have some sort of way to write down what you are selling. One great tool is a simple spreadsheet. If you use spreadsheets, you can put all of your sales in one place.

Try using google sheets so you don't lose it if your computer decides it has had enough.

If you put your numbers into Excel, it helps you come up with your total sales and discover patterns. You can use this information to create graphs so that you are able to visually understand the data.

It is always a good idea to save your receipts. If you save your receipts, you will always know how much you were spending on your business. You can later type these numbers into a program like Excel. If you do not save receipts, you may forget about some charges. This might be basic information but it's worthwhile to mention it.

If you forget about even one charge, your numbers will be off which the IRS doesn't like. If you are not able to track how much you were spending, it can lead to pretty bad consequences.

Saving receipts is fairly simple, it is something that you should always do for your business. Consider using one place to store your receipts and put them in as soon as you receive them.

Make a separate banking account for the business so your own bank account isn't mixed with the business bank account. This clears up a whole lot of unnecessary headaches during tax season.

Your business might make a profit but don't forget that your time is also worth money. Consider starting this as a side hustle and i everything works out, you can go full time.

FAQs and Tips

We have covered quite a lot of information in this book so far.

Let's look into questions I commonly get asked through email.

"How long can I store my seeds?"

Typically, seeds should only be stored for two years. There are certain types of seeds that can be stored for up to four to six years, but this is not always a good idea. The best choice is to use your seeds within two years from when you bought them. This is good news because when you do not need to use them right away, they do last quite a long time. If you have had seeds sitting around for more than two years, you may want to consider doing a germination test again to see if they still perform above 80%.

"Why are my greens turning yellow?"

If your greens are turning yellow, it means that they need more direct sunlight or artificial light. You can do this by making sure that your plants are next to a window or that you have adequate lighting on them. If you do not have adequate light shining on them then you will not be able to successfully grow a crop.

If your plants are turning yellow, it means they are not able to do the photosynthesis that they need to be doing. This will eventually cause your plants to die before they produce anything that you can eat.

"Is hydroponics better than soil for microgreens?"

The answer is no, most of the time it's not. Hydroponics is not the best way to grow most microgreens. Fellow growers are reporting that hydroponics works for them. I haven't found it worthwhile to move from soil to hydroponics for the reasons I talked about earlier.

"Can I regrow microgreens after cutting?"

Yes, with certain microgreens you can do this, but not all will regrow properly and this will result in a wilted second yield. My recommendation: don't bother. You are better off using the tray for the next growing cycle where you can harvest more and better-looking microgreens.

What is live packaging?

Live packaging includes the microgreens together with the roots and grow media. This way the microgreens can be stored longer. Some stores and restaurants don't accept anything containing a soil mix. Talk to your buyers and ask them what they prefer.

Are pea sprouts and pea shoots the same?

No, they are not. Sprouts are harvested early before cotyledon leaves appear. while shoots will be harvested when the first true leaves appear depending on taste.

What is a 10x20 tray of microgreens worth?

This depends on your location together with supply and demand. Visit a local farmers market and see if anyone is selling microgreens there.

The profit from selling at the farmers market will be higher for one tray compared to restaurants or grocery stores. This is because at the grocery store you also pay for space to sell your products. Restaurants buy higher quantities at a lower price than the farmers market.

From the previously mentioned study, we know you can get a price from $2 to $6 per ounce and the yield is 1.5 to 4 ounces per square foot. One 10x20 tray is 1.4ft^2. The yield will be 2.1 to 5.6 ounces. Which is $4.2 to $33.6 without costs. You see that this is very broad and quite impossible to give you an estimate without knowing the market value.

At what temperature should I store my microgreens?

Your microgreens should be stored when they are dry at a temperature of 38-40°F or 3-5°C.

I'm a restaurant owner and I want to grow microgreens in the kitchen. What's the best way to do this?

The best way to grow microgreens in a commercial kitchen is by using a hydroponics method without the nutrients. Use 10x20 or 10x10 trays and use the same process as I discussed but swap the potting mix with bio felt.

I see some people soaking the seeds in bleach before seeding. Should I do that too?

No, the seeds are already contamination free. If you run into problems with germination rate you can try to soak them in a 3% bleach solution and see if the germination rate improves. If germination does not improve you should try another supplier.

Can microgreens help with weight loss?

Yes, they are very nutrient-dense and low in calories. They contain 1 gram of fiber per ounce which will keep you full for longer. Generally eating green leafy vegetables is good for weight loss.

Now that we have answered my most frequently asked questions, let's move into some other tips that I have for you.

My first tip would be to buy seeds in bulk. This is because you need a lot of seeds and you can keep them for quite some time. Your profit margins will be higher if you can buy in bulk. Even if you're growing microgreens for fun, you will still spend a lot of money on seeds. Once you start planting them, you'll realize how many seeds you really need to use each time.

I recommend that you test the germination rate of your seed supplier first before you order in bulk from that supplier.

If you are planning on just starting out a business in microgreens you may want to start with a small side business at first. Tha way, you don't waste a lot of money if your business doesn' work out as you intended. It also allows you to get to know microgreens and how to grow them. It is almost always a good idea to start small than to start big.

Next, let's look into the most profitable types of microgreens. I you are looking to start out selling microgreens and you wer wondering which kinds to plant to make the most money, you should know that sunflowers, pea, broccoli, and radishe typically sell the most.

Another good tip for your business is to make a standard operating procedure for every action you perform. Your SOP can teach you what you need to do every day, so you do not forget anything, and you do not need to spend time trying to remember certain things. If you are going on vacation, it's easy to hand it over to a friend so he or she can take care of your greens for several days without having to call you all the time.

If you want your setup to start small, you may want to consider making it expandable so that when your business grows, you are able to fit more trays. If you start with a small space, you may not have enough money to pay for a different space later, but you also do not want to pay for a place that is too big if you may not ever need it. Because of this, having a space that is expandable is the best option.

One of the most important tips that I can give you for your business is to network. Connections and a good reputation are crucial for long-term contracts. They can get you new customers and help you to keep the ones that you already have. When you treat customers well, they spread the word about you. You need your clients and customers to stick around and you need new ones, so having a good reputation is the best thing you can do for your business.

When your business starts to become sturdy, you can start to predict what you will need to plant. This will help you to save money because you will only be planting the things that you know will be purchased instead of things that will not be purchased and will end up not being used.

It will help you to avoid spending money that you don't need to spend. It may take a little bit of thought to figure out what to plant and when to plant it so that your customer has it at the right time, but it will be worth it in the end.

Even if you predict what your customer wants, sometimes, things will come up. Your customer may not want them, or your crop may fail, and you won't be able to provide to them what they need.

If you have a failed crop, you need to make sure that you tell your customers right away. Call them when you know that the crop is going to fail and let them know that their order won't be ready in time, and you will be refunding them or that the order will be late.

The most important thing in this situation is to have good customer service. Not providing what the customer wants is never a good situation, but if you handle it well, it will go better than if you do not have clear communication and a plan set up to keep your customers happy. Consider offering them another microgreen for free to make up for the inconvenience.

If you cannot provide what the customer wants and you do not treat them well in the process, you may lose them as a customer

Final Words

You have come to the end of the book! I hope you learned a thing or two in the process. Now, let's grow these delicious and healthy microgreens together!

Share your progress pictures on the Facebook group:

- **https://practicalgrowing.com/facebook**

Or visit my website for more information:

- **https://practicalgrowing.com**

If you have issues or suggestions, please write an email to the following email address:

- **contact@practicalgrowing.com**

Happy growing!

Microgreens Journal

You can use the following journal entries as a template to note your findings after every harvest. Using these journals will increase your yield to reach its full potential, giving you more profit and more microgreens.

Variety			
Soaked?			
Sown date			
Blackout time			
Seed density			
Date of harvest			
Total days to harvest			
Harvest weight			
Mold problems?			

Variety			
Soaked?			
Sown date			
Blackout time			
Seed density			
Date of harvest			
Total days to harvest			
Harvest weight			

Variety			
Soaked?			
Sown date			
Blackout time			
Seed density			
Date of harvest			
Total days to harvest			
Harvest weight			

Variety			
Soaked?			
Sown date			
Blackout time			
Seed density			
Date of harvest			
Total days to harvest			
Harvest weight			

Variety			
Soaked?			
Sown date			
Blackout time			
Seed density			
Date of harvest			
Total days to harvest			
Harvest weight			

Variety			
Soaked?			
Sown date			
Blackout time			
Seed density			
Date of harvest			
Total days to harvest			
Harvest weight			

Variety			
Soaked?			
Sown date			
Blackout time			
Seed density			
Date of harvest			
Total days to harvest			
Harvest weight			

Variety			
Soaked?			
Sown date			
Blackout time			
Seed density			
Date of harvest			
Total days to harvest			
Harvest weight			

Variety			
Soaked?			
Sown date			
Blackout time			
Seed density			
Date of harvest			
Total days to harvest			
Harvest weight			

Notes

Made in the USA
Coppell, TX
29 December 2019

13860549R00061